CONTEMPORA

READING AND WRITING HANDBOOKS

INTRODUCTORY WORD BOOK

EDWARD FRY, PH.D.

CB

CONTEMPORARY BOOKS

a division of NTC/CONTEMPORARY PUBLISHING GROUP
Lincolnwood, Illinois USA

ISBN: 0-8092-0877-6

Published by Contemporary Books,
a division of NTC/Contemporary Publishing Group, Inc.,
4255 West Touhy Avenue,
Lincolnwood (Chicago), Illinois 60646-1975 U.S.A.

8 9 0 GW 11 10 9 8 7 6 5 4 3

Director, New Product Development
Noreen Lopez

Editorial Manager
Cynthia Krejcsi

Project Editor
Christine Kelner

Design and Production Manager
Norma Underwood

Production Artist
Thomas D. Scharf

Cover and Interior Design
Kristy Sheldon

INTRODUCTION

This book gives the 1,000 most common words from the Instant Word list* in alphabetical order so that student writers can quickly find how to spell them. These words make up more than 90 percent of all written material. Also included are additional words that are common and important in adult experience and situations, such as the word *license* or *deposit*. However, students should also add their own words that they need in writing. These might be words they have asked someone how to spell, words misspelled on a previous story, or words used in a particular subject of interest.

Help the student writer to find words. Point out that if just the first two letters are known, then the word should be easy to find. Use the thumb index on the margin of right-hand pages and the two-letter alpha groupings on left-hand pages (word pages) to make the student's search easier.

Encourage students to look up words, not ask someone how to spell them, and to add new words when a word they seek is not on the list.

CONTENTS

* (found in *1000 Instant Words*, Reading and Writing Handbooks)

A Words

ab
able
about
above

ac
accident
across
act
action
actually

ad
add
addition
adjective

af
afraid
Africa
after
afternoon

ag
again
against
age
ago
agreed

ah
ahead

ai
air

al
all
allow
almost
alone
along
already
also
although
always

am
am
America
among
amount

an
an
and
angle
animal
another
answer
any
anything

ap
appear
apple

ar
are
area
arms
army
around
arrived
art

as
as
ask
aspirin

at
at

aw
away

Write your own *A* words on the next page. ▶

Personal *A* Words _____

A	a
B	b
C	c
D	d
E	e
F	f
G	g
H	h
I	i
J	j
K	k
L	l
M	m
N	n
O	o
P	p
Q	q
R	r
S	s
T	t
U	u
V	v
W	w
X	x
Y	y
Z	z

B WORDS

ba

baby
babysitter
back
bad
ball
bank
base

be

be
bear
beat
beautiful
became
because
become
bed
been
before
began
begin
behind
being
believe
bell
belong
below
beside

best
better
between

bi

big
bill
birds
bit

bl

black
block
blood
blow
blue

bo

board
boat
body
bones
book
born
boss
both
bottom
bought
box
boy

br

branches
bread
break
breakfast
bright
bring
British
broken
brother
brought
brown

bu

build
building
built
burning
bus
business
but
buy

by

by

Write your own *B* words on the next page. ▶

PERSONAL *B* WORDS _____

A	a
B	b
C	c
D	d
E	e
F	f
G	g
H	h
I	i
J	j
K	k
L	l
M	m
N	n
O	o
P	p
Q	q
R	r
S	s
T	t
U	u
V	v
W	w
X	x
Y	y
Z	z

C WORDS

ca
call
came
can
cannot
can't
capital
captain
car
care
carefully
carry
case
cat
catch
cattle
caught
cause

ce
cells
center
cents
century
cereal
certain

ch
chance
change
chart
check
chicken
chief
child
children
choose
church

ci
circle
city

cl
class
clean
clear
climbed
clinic
close
clothes
cloud

co
coast
coffee
cold
color
column
come
common
company
compare
complete
compound
conditions
consider
consonant
contain
continued
control
cook
cool
copy
corn
corner
correct
cost
cotton
could
couldn't
count
country
course
covered
cows

cr
create
credit
cried
crops
cross
crowd

cu
current
cut

car

Write your own *C* words on the next page. ▶

Personal *C* Words _____

_____	_____
_____	_____
_____	_____
_____	_____
_____	_____
_____	_____
_____	_____
_____	_____
_____	_____
_____	_____
_____	_____
_____	_____
_____	_____
_____	_____
_____	_____
_____	_____
_____	_____

A	a
B	b
C	**c**
D	d
E	e
F	f
G	g
H	h
I	i
J	j
K	k
L	l
M	m
N	n
O	o
P	p
Q	q
R	r
S	s
T	t
U	u
V	v
W	w
X	x
Y	y
Z	z

D WORDS

da
dance
dark
day
daycare

de
dead
deal
death
decided
decimal
deep
dentist
deposit
describe
desert
design
details
determine
developed

di
dictionary
did
didn't
died
difference
different
difficult
dinner

direct
direction
discovered
distance
divided
division

do
do
doctor
does
doesn't
dog
dollars
done
don't
door
down
dozen

dr
draw
drawing
dress
drive
drop
drugstore
dry

du
during

dollars

Write your own *D* words on the next page. ▶

Personal *D* Words

_____   _____

_____   _____

_____   _____

_____   _____

_____   _____

_____   _____

_____   _____

_____   _____

_____   _____

_____   _____

_____   _____

_____   _____

_____   _____

_____   _____

_____   _____

_____   _____

A	a
B	b
C	c
D	d
E	e
F	f
G	g
H	h
I	i
J	j
K	k
L	l
M	m
N	n
O	o
P	p
Q	q
R	r
S	s
T	t
U	u
V	v
W	w
X	x
Y	y
Z	z

E WORDS

ea

each
early
ears
earth
east
easy
eat

ed

edge

ef

effect

eg

eggs

ei

eight
either

el

electric
elements
elevator
else

em

emergency
employee

en

end
energy
engine
England
English
enjoy
enough
entered
entire

eq

equal
equation
equipment

es

especially

eu

Europe

ev

even
evening
ever
every
everyone
everything

ex

exactly
example
except
exciting
exercise
expect
experience
experiment
explain
express

ey

eye

Write your own *E* words on the next page. ▶

Personal *E* Words _____

A	a
B	b
C	c
D	d
E	e
F	f
G	g
H	h
I	i
J	j
K	k
L	l
M	m
N	n
O	o
P	p
Q	q
R	r
S	s
T	t
U	u
V	v
W	w
X	x
Y	y
Z	z

F WORDS

fa

face
fact
factories
factors
fair
fall
family
famous
far
farm
farmers
fast
father

fe

fear
feel
feeling
feet
fell
felt
fever
few

fi

field
fig
fight
figure
filled
finally
find
fine
fingers
finished
fire
first
fish
fit
five

fl

flat
floor
flour
flowers
flu
fly

fo

follow
food
foot
for
force
forest
form
forward
found
four

fr

fraction
France
free
French
fresh
friends
from
front
fruit
fry

fu

full
fun

Write your own *F* words on the next page. ▶

PERSONAL *F* WORDS _____

A	a
B	b
C	c
D	d
E	e
F	**f**
G	g
H	h
I	i
J	j
K	k
L	l
M	m
N	n
O	o
P	p
Q	q
R	r
S	s
T	t
U	u
V	v
W	w
X	x
Y	y
Z	z

G Words

ga

gallon
game
garden
garlic
gas
gave

ge

general
get

gi

gift
girl
give

gl

glass

go

go
God
gold
gone
good
got
government

gr

grapes
grass
grease
great
Greek
green
grew
grocery
ground
group
grow

gu

guess
gum
gun

gy

gym

gold

Write your own *G* words on the next page. ▶

PERSONAL G WORDS

A	a
B	b
C	c
D	d
E	e
F	f
G	g
H	h
I	i
J	j
K	k
L	l
M	m
N	n
O	o
P	p
Q	q
R	r
S	s
T	t
U	u
V	v
W	w
X	x
Y	y
Z	z

H WORDS

ha
had
hair
half
ham
hand
happened
happy
hard
has
hat
have

he
he
head
headache
hear
heard
heart
heat
heavy
held
help
her
here

hi
high
hill
him
himself
his
history
hit

ho
hold
hole
home
honey

hope
horse
hospital
hot
hours
house
how
however

hu
huge
human
hundred
hunting
husband

house

Write your own *H* words on the next page. ▶

Personal *H* Words

A	a
B	b
C	c
D	d
E	e
F	f
G	g
H	**h**
I	i
J	j
K	k
L	l
M	m
N	n
O	o
P	p
Q	q
R	r
S	s
T	t
U	u
V	v
W	w
X	x
Y	y
Z	z

I Words

I
> I
> I'll

ic
> ice

id
> idea

if
> if

il
> ill

im
> important

in
> in
> inches
> include
> increase
> Indian
> indicate
> industry
> information
> insects
> inside
> instead
> instruments
> interest

> interesting
> into

ir
> iron

is
> is
> island
> isn't

it
> it
> itch
> it's
> itself

island

Write your own *I* words on the next page. ▶

Personal *I* Words _____

_____	_____			A	a
_____	_____			B	b
_____	_____			C	c
_____	_____			D	d
_____	_____			E	e

J Words

ja
jail
jam
Japanese

je
jelly

jo
job
joined

ju
juice
jumped
just

K Words

ke
keep
kept
key

ki
kid
killed
kind
king
kitchen

kn
knee
knew
knife
know
known

key

Write your own *J* and *K* words on the next page. ▶

Personal *J* and *K* Words _____

A	a
B	b
C	c
D	d
E	e
F	f
G	g
H	h
I	i
J	j
K	k
L	l
M	m
N	n
O	o
P	p
Q	q
R	r
S	s
T	t
U	u
V	v
W	w
X	x
Y	y
Z	z

L WORDS

la
lady
lake
land
language
large
last
late
laughed
laundry
law
lay

le
lead
learn
least
leave
led
left
legs
length
less
let
let's
letter
level

li
license
lie
life
lifted
light
like
line
list
listen
little
live

lo
loan
located
long
look
lost
lot
loud
love
low

lu
lunch

lady

Write your own *L* words on the next page. ▶

PERSONAL *L* WORDS _____

_____ _____

_____ _____

_____ _____

_____ _____

_____ _____

_____ _____

_____ _____

_____ _____

_____ _____

_____ _____

_____ _____

_____ _____

_____ _____

_____ _____

_____ _____

_____ _____

_____ _____

A	a
B	b
C	c
D	d
E	e
F	f
G	g
H	h
I	i
J	j
K	k
L	l
M	m
N	n
O	o
P	p
Q	q
R	r
S	s
T	t
U	u
V	v
W	w
X	x
Y	y
Z	z

M WORDS

ma
machine
made
mail
main
major
make
man
manager
many
map
march
margarine
mark
match
material
matter
may
maybe

me
me
meal
mean
measure
meat
medicine
meet
melody

members
men
metal
method

mi
middle
might
mile
milk
million
mind
mine
minutes
miss

mo
modern
molecules
moment
money
months
moon
more
morning
mortgage
most
mother
mountain
mouth

move
movement
movie

mu
much
music
must

my
my

Write your own *M* words on the next page. ▶

PERSONAL *M* WORDS _____

A	a
B	b
C	c
D	d
E	e
F	f
G	g
H	h
I	i
J	j
K	k
L	l
M	**m**
N	n
O	o
P	p
Q	q
R	r
S	s
T	t
U	u
V	v
W	w
X	x
Y	y
Z	z

N WORDS

na

name
nation
natural

ne

near
necessary
need
never
new
newspaper
next

ni

nice
night
nine

no

no
nor
north
northern
nose
not
note
nothing
notice
noun
now

nu

number
numeral
nurse

note

Write your own *N* words on the next page. ▶

Personal *N* Words _____

_____   _____

_____   _____

_____   _____

_____   _____

_____   _____

_____   _____

_____   _____

_____   _____

_____   _____

_____   _____

_____   _____

_____   _____

_____   _____

_____   _____

A	a
B	b
C	c
D	d
E	e
F	f
G	g
H	h
I	i
J	j
K	k
L	l
M	m
N	n
O	o
P	p
Q	q
R	r
S	s
T	t
U	u
V	v
W	w
X	x
Y	y
Z	z

O WORDS

ob
- object
- observe

oc
- ocean

of
- of
- off
- office
- often

oh
- oh

oi
- oil

ol
- old

on
- on
- once
- one
- only

op
- open
- operation
- opposite

or
- or
- orange
- order

ot
- other

ou
- our
- out
- outside

ov
- over
- overtime

ow
- owe
- own

ox
- oxygen

ocean

Write your own *O* words on the next page. ▶

Personal *O* Words

A	a
B	b
C	c
D	d
E	e
F	f
G	g
H	h
I	i
J	j
K	k
L	l
M	m
N	n
O	o
P	p
Q	q
R	r
S	s
T	t
U	u
V	v
W	w
X	x
Y	y
Z	z

P WORDS

pa

page
paint
pair
paper
paragraph
park
part
particular
party
passed
past
patient
pattern
pay

pe

pear
people
per
perhaps
period
person

ph

phrase

pi

picked
picture
piece
pizza

pl

place
plains
plan
plane
planets
plant
play
please
plural

po

poem
point
poison
pole
police
poor
position
possible
post office
pounds
power

pr

practice
prepared
preschool
prescription

present
president
pretty
price
printed
probably
problem
process
produce
products
property
provide

pu

pulled
pushed
put

Write your own *P* words on the next page. ▶

PERSONAL *P* WORDS _____

A	a
B	b
C	c
D	d
E	e
F	f
G	g
H	h
I	i
J	j
K	k
L	l
M	m
N	n
O	o
P	p
Q	q
R	r
S	s
T	t
U	u
V	v
W	w
X	x
Y	y
Z	z

Q Words

qu

quart
questions
quickly
quiet
quit
quite

R Words

ra

race
radio
rain
raised
ran
rather

re

reached
read
ready
real
reason
received
record
red
refund
region
remain
remember
rent
repair
repeated
report
represent
rest
result
return

rh

rhythm

ri

rice
rich
ride

right
ring
rise
river

ro

road
rock
rolled
room
root
rope
rose
round
row

ru

rule
run

Write your own *Q* and *R* words on the next page. ▶

Personal *Q* and *R* Words

A	a
B	b
C	c
D	d
E	e
F	f
G	g
H	h
I	i
J	j
K	k
L	l
M	m
N	n
O	o
P	p
Q	q
R	r
S	s
T	t
U	u
V	v
W	w
X	x
Y	y
Z	z

S WORDS

sa
safe
said
sail
same
sand
sat
save
saw
say

sc
scale
school
science
scientists
score

se
sea
seat
second
section
see
seeds
seem
seen
sell
send
sense
sent
sentence
separate
serve
set
settled
seven
several

sh
shall

shape
sharp
she
ship
shoes
shop
short
should
shoulder
shouted
show
shown

si
sick
side
sight
sign
silent
similar
simple
since
sing
single
sir
sister
sit
six
size

sk
skin
sky

sl
sleep
slowly

sm
small
smell
smiled

sn
snow

so
so
soft
soil
soldier
solution
solve
some
someone
something
sometimes
son
song
soon
sound
south
southern

sp
space
speak
special
speed
spell
spot
spread
spring

sq
square

st
stand
stars
start
state
statement
stay
steel

step
stick
still
stone
stood
stop
store
story
straight
strange
stream
street
stretched
string
strong
students
study

su
subject
substances
such
suddenly
suffix
sugar
suggested
sum
summer
sun
supply
suppose
sure
surface
surprise

sw
swim

sy
syllables
symbols
system

Write your own *S* words on the next page. ▶

PERSONAL S WORDS

_____

A	a
B	b
C	c
D	d
E	e
F	f
G	g
H	h
I	i
J	j
K	k
L	l
M	m
N	n
O	o
P	p
Q	q
R	r
S	**s**
T	t
U	u
V	v
W	w
X	x
Y	y
Z	z

T WORDS

ta
table
tail
take
talk
tall

te
teacher
team
telephone
television
tell
temperature
ten
terms
test

th
than
that
the
their
them
themselves
then
there
thermometer
these
they
thick
thin
thing
think
third
this
those
though
thought
thousands
three
through
thus

ti
ticket
tied
time
tiny

to
to
today
together
told
tone
too
took
tools
toothpaste
top
total
touch
toward
town

tr
track
trade
train
travel
tree
triangle
trip
trouble
truck
true
try

tu
tube
turkey
turn

tw
two

ty
type

Write your own *T* words on the next page. ▶

PERSONAL *T* WORDS

A	a
B	b
C	c
D	d
E	e
F	f
G	g
H	h
I	i
J	j
K	k
L	l
M	m
N	n
O	o
P	p
Q	q
R	r
S	s
T	t
U	u
V	v
W	w
X	x
Y	y
Z	z

U WORDS

ug
ugly

un
uncle
under
underline
understand
unfair
uniform
unit
until

up
up
upon

us
us
use
usually

Write your own *U* words on the next page. ▶

Personal *U* Words _____

A	a
B	b
C	c
D	d
E	e
F	f
G	g
H	h
I	i
J	j
K	k
L	l
M	m
N	n
O	o
P	p
Q	q
R	r
S	s
T	t
U	u
V	v
W	w
X	x
Y	y
Z	z

V WORDS

va
vacation
valley
value
vanilla
various

ve
vegetable
verb
very

vi
view
village
vinegar
virus
visit
vitamins

vo
voice
vowel

valley

Write your own *V* words on the next page. ▶

PERSONAL *V* WORDS _____

A	a
B	b
C	c
D	d
E	e
F	f
G	g
H	h
I	i
J	j
K	k
L	l
M	m
N	n
O	o
P	p
Q	q
R	r
S	s
T	t
U	ü
V	v
W	w
X	x
Y	y
Z	z

W WORDS

wa

wait
walk
wall
want
war
warm
was
wash
Washington
wasn't
watch
water
waves
way

we

we
wear
weather
week
weight
well
we'll
went
were
west
western

wh

what
wheels
when
where
whether
which
while
white
who
whole
whose
why

wi

wide
wife
wild
will
win
wind
window
wings
winter
wire
wish
with

within
without

wo

woman
women
wonder
won't
wood
word
work
workers
world
would
wouldn't

wr

write
written
wrong
wrote

Write your own *W* words on the next page. ▶

Personal *W* Words _____

_____ _____

_____ _____

_____ _____

_____ _____

_____ _____

_____ _____

_____ _____

_____ _____

_____ _____

_____ _____

_____ _____

_____ _____

_____ _____

_____ _____

A	a
B	b
C	c
D	d
E	e
F	f
G	g
H	h
I	i
J	j
K	k
L	l
M	m
N	n
O	o
P	p
Q	q
R	r
S	s
T	t
U	u
V	v
W	w
X	x
Y	y
Z	z

X Words _____

x-ray

Y Words _____

ya
yard

ye
year
yellow
yes
yet

yo
you
young
your
you're
yourself

Z Words _____

ze
zero

zi
zip code

zo
zoo

Write your own *X*, *Y*, and *Z* words on the next page. ▶

Personal *X*, *Y*, and *Z* Words

A	a
B	b
C	c
D	d
E	e
F	f
G	g
H	h
I	i
J	j
K	k
L	l
M	m
N	n
O	o
P	p
Q	q
R	r
S	s
T	t
U	u
V	v
W	w
X	x
Y	y
Z	z

PICTURE NOUNS

Use the following words to write stories. These picture words also suggest story ideas or story expansion.

boy

girl

man

woman

baby

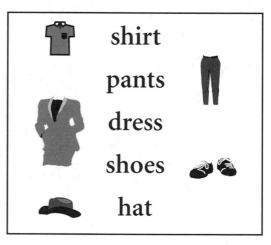

shirt

pants

dress

shoes

hat

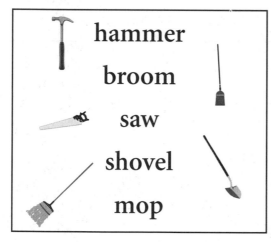

hammer

broom

saw

shovel

mop

cat

dog

bird

fish

rabbit

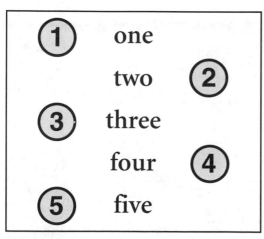

1 one

two 2

3 three

four 4

5 five

Picture Nouns

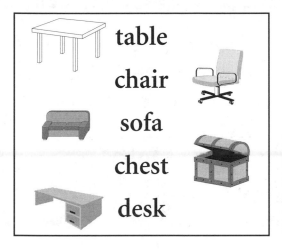

table

chair

sofa

chest

desk

bread

meat

soup

egg

salad

cup

plate

bowl

fork

spoon

water

milk

juice

soda

tea

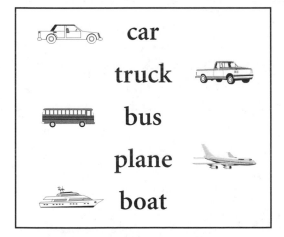

car

truck

bus

plane

boat

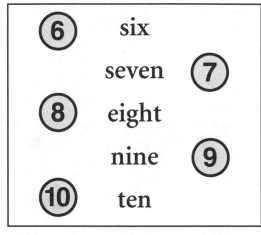

6 six

seven **7**

8 eight

nine **9**

10 ten

sun

moon

star

cloud

rain

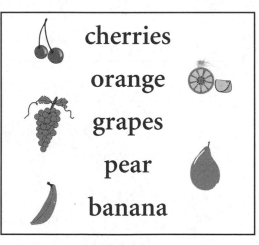

cherries

orange

grapes

pear

banana

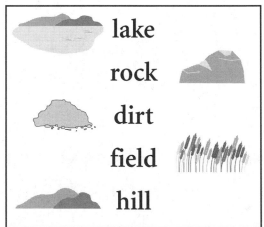

lake

rock

dirt

field

hill

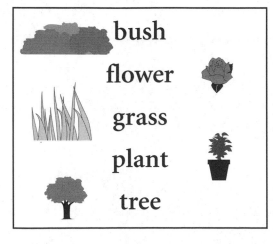

bush

flower

grass

plant

tree

horse

cow

pig

chicken

duck

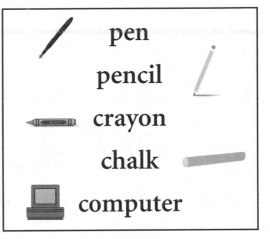

pen

pencil

crayon

chalk

computer

farmer

police

cook

doctor

teacher

book

newspaper

magazine

sign

letter

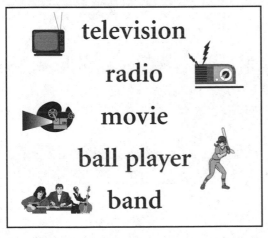

television

radio

movie

ball player

band

HANDWRITING CHART/ZANER-BLOSER

Zaner-Bloser Manuscript Alphabet (Printing)

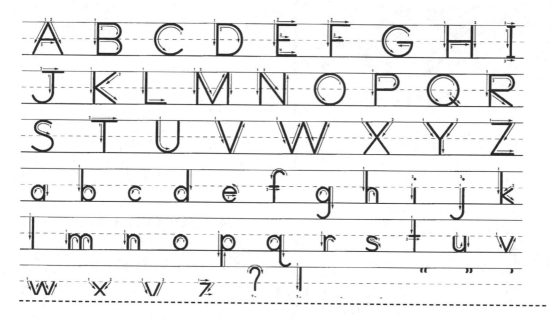

Zaner-Bloser Cursive Alphabet (Handwriting)

Handwriting Chart/D'Nealian

D'Nealian™ Manuscript Alphabet (Printing)

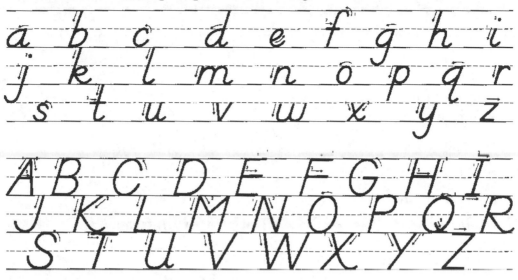

D'Nealian™ Cursive Alphabet (Handwriting)

D'Nealian™ Numbers

0 1 2 3 4 5 6 7 8 9

PHONICS

This page has all of the common sounds used in English. The most common way the sound is written (spelled) is given. For example, the most common way to write the short /a/ sound is with the letter *a* as in *hat*.

short a *hat*
long a *age*
a (*air* sound) *care*
broad a *father*
b *bad*
ch *child*
d *did*
short e *let*
long e *bee*
er (or short *u* plus *r*) *her*
f *fat*
g *go*
h *he*
wh *wheat*
short i *bit*
long i *ice*
j *jam*
k *kind*
kw *quick*
l *land*
m *me*
n *no*
ng (blend) *long*

short o *hot*
long o *open*
broad o *off*
oi *boil*
ou *house*
p *pen*
r *run*
s *say*
sh *she*
t *tell*
th (voiceless) *thin*
th (voiced) *then*
short u *cup*
short oo *good*
long u *use*
long oo *loose*
v *very*
w *will*
y (consonant) *you*
z *zero*
zh *measure*
schwa sound *alone, silent, direct, pencil, onion, circus*

SPELLING RULES

Plurals and S Forms of Verbs

A. Add -*s* to most nouns and verbs:
   cows, runs

B. Add -*es* if the word ends in *ch, sh, x, s,* or *z*:
   box—boxes; rush—rushes

For words ending in *y*

C. If the word ends in a *y* after a consonant (not a vowel), change the
   y to *i* and add -*es*:
   baby—babies; cry—cries

Adding Endings and Suffixes

A. **Basic Rule:** Just add the ending or suffix.
   Regular examples: *want—wanted, wanting, wants*

B. Exceptions
   For words ending in *e*: Drop the final *e* if the ending or suffix begins
   with a vowel:
   rose—rosy; name—naming, named
   For words ending in *y*: Change the *y* to *i* if *y* comes after a consonant:
   carry—carried (ending here is -*ed.*)

Prefixes

Basic Rule: Prefixes never change spelling. They are just added to
   whole words.
   un- + happy = unhappy

Compound Words

Basic Rule: Keep the full spelling of both words. Just join them
   together without a hyphen.
   ear + ring = earring; room + mate = roommate

airline	haircut
backyard	pancake
blackboard	postcard
bluebird	shipwreck
campfire	softball
football	washcloth

Homophones

Homophones are words that sound the same but are spelled differently and have a different meaning. Some people call these words *homonyms*. They are important to writers because using them incorrectly causes many spelling errors.

to (toward)
I went <u>to</u> school.

too (also)
My dog went to school, <u>too</u>.

two (number)
My son is in grade <u>two</u>.

there (a place)
Put the book over <u>there</u>.

their (pronoun)
It is <u>their</u> book.

they're (they are)
<u>They're</u> not going to work.

no (negative)
She said, "<u>No</u>, I will not go."

know (familiar with)
He did not <u>know</u> how to drive.

by (near)
We live <u>by</u> the river.

buy (purchase)
Let's <u>buy</u> some groceries.

our (pronoun)
He lives on <u>our</u> street.

hour (time)
The lesson takes one <u>hour</u>.

I (pronoun)
<u>I</u> don't like it.

eye (what you use to see)
She got sand in her <u>eye</u>.

aunt (relative)
My <u>aunt</u> lives next door.

ant (insect)
There is an <u>ant</u> in the jam.

hole (opening)
There is a <u>hole</u> in the wall.

whole (complete)
He ate the <u>whole</u> pie.

ate (food)
She <u>ate</u> the whole pie.

eight (number)
He has <u>eight</u> basketballs.

cent (money)
Don't pay one <u>cent</u> more.

sent (did send)
I <u>sent</u> you a letter yesterday.

be (verb)
When will you <u>be</u> home?

bee (insect)
That <u>bee</u> can sting you.

Word Variety

Synonyms

A synonym is a word with the same or almost the same meaning as another word.

all – every
ask – question
back – rear
below – under
boy – young man, guy
call – yell
car – auto
close – shut
fat – plump
happy – glad
high – tall
large – big
like – enjoy
little – small
make – build
new – fresh
open – unlocked
pain – hurt
put – place
speed – hurry
thief – crook
tiny – small
world – earth
write – record

Mood Words

Angry

mean	rude
nasty	wicked

Sad

hurt	alone
sore	awful
blue	

Happy

joy	glad
funny	cheerful
pleased	

Nice

fair	peaceful
polite	warm
caring	

Amount Words

few	empty
lots	many
much	

Sound Words

loud	silent
soft	noisy
bang	

Punctuation

Period

1. At the end of a sentence: *He asked what time it was.*
2. After abbreviations: *Mr., U.S.A.*

Question Mark

1. At the end of a question: *What time is it?*

Apostrophe

1. To show possession: *Bill's job*
2. Letters or numbers left out: *isn't, '96*

Quotation Marks

1. Exact words: *She said, "Hello."*
2. Titles of songs and stories: *He read "The Gold Bug."*
3. Special words or slang: *He is "nuts."*
4. Direct quote: *He told me that he "never lied."*

Comma

1. Series: *She likes clothes, movies, and sports.*
   The big, bad, ugly wolf howled.
2. Before real speech: *She said, "Hello."*
3. Dates: *July 4, 1776*
4. Titles: *Joe Smith, Ph.D.*
5. Informal letter greeting: *Dear Danita,*
6. Letter closing: *Yours truly,*
7. Last name first: *Smith, Joe*
8. To separate city and state: *Los Angeles, California*

Exclamation Point

1. To show strong emotion: *She is the best!*
2. After interjections: *Help!*

CAPITALIZATION

Use a capital letter for:

A. Proper nouns

1. **Names:** Aaron, Maria

2. **Titles:** Mr. Smith, Ms. Adams, Dr. Jones

3. **Countries, cities, and states:** United States, Boston, Michigan

4. **Streets:** Hill St., First Avenue

5. **Days, months:** Thursday, April

6. **Schools and companies:** Elmore Community College, Nabisco

7. **Holidays:** Christmas, Fourth of July

B. The first word in a sentence

My dog hates my cat.

C. The first word in each line of most poetry

It was many and many a year ago,
In a kingdom by the sea,
That a maiden there lived whom you may know
By the name of ANNABEL LEE;
And this maiden she lived with no other thought
Than to love and be loved by me.

(Edgar Allen Poe, "Annabel Lee")

D. All main words in a title

The new book is *Like Water for Chocolate.*
"The Gift of the Magi" is a good story.

U.S. Post Office Authorized State Abbreviations (Note: No periods)

U.S. Territory Abbreviations

Alabama	AL
Alaska	AK
American Samoa	AS
Arizona	AZ
Arkansas	AR
California	CA
Canal Zone	CZ
Colorado	CO
Connecticut	CT
Delaware	DE
District of Columbia	DC
Florida	FL
Georgia	GA
Guam	GU
Hawaii	HI
Idaho	ID
Illinois	IL
Indiana	IN
Iowa	IA
Kansas	KS
Kentucky	KY
Louisiana	LA
Maine	ME
Maryland	MD
Massachusetts	MA
Michigan	MI
Minnesota	MN
Mississippi	MS
Missouri	MO
Montana	MT
Nebraska	NE
Nevada	NV
New Hampshire	NH
New Jersey	NJ
New Mexico	NM
New York	NY
North Carolina	NC
North Dakota	ND
Ohio	OH
Oklahoma	OK
Oregon	OR
Pennsylvania	PA
Puerto Rico	PR
Rhode Island	RI
South Carolina	SC
South Dakota	SD
Tennessee	TN
Texas	TX
Utah	UT
Vermont	VT
Virginia	VA
Virgin Islands	VI
Washington	WA
West Virginia	WV
Wisconsin	WI
Wyoming	WY

Months

January	Jan.
February	Feb.
March	Mar.
April	Apr.
May	May
June	June
July	July
August	Aug.
September	Sept.
October	Oct.
November	Nov.
December	Dec.

Days of the Week

Sunday	Sun.
Monday	Mon.
Tuesday	Tues.
Wednesday	Wed.
Thursday	Thurs.
Friday	Fri.
Saturday	Sat.

LETTER FORM

Informal Letter

sender's address	473 West St. Klamath Falls, OR 97625 Aug. 2, 1998
greeting	Dear Elena,
body	I am having so much fun this summer. The lake is beautiful. I miss you. I'll see you back at work soon.
closing	Your friend,
signature	Benita

Envelope

return (sender's) address	Benita Hunt 473 West St. Klamath Falls, OR 97625
	stamp
receiver's address	Elena Flores 1614 N. Burns Dr. Santa Monica, CA 90405

SENTENCE BUILDING

To build a sentence, select a word or phrase from each column:

SUBJECT	VERB	OBJECT OR PHRASE
A small boy	swam	the tree
The fish	climbed	the deer
The hunter	killed	over the fence
The long train	jumped	to the students
A teacher	carried	the mountain
A snake	moved	to the story
My good friend	lives	into the water
The big truck	read	down the street
The workers	listened	a heavy load
The woman	found	in the desert

You can choose more words to make your sentences read better or add interest.

STORY STARTERS

Titles

If I Ruled the World
A Home of My Own
Curing the Blues
My Neighborhood
The Best Thing To Eat
A Great Movie
A Family Memory
An Exciting Day
The Perfect Job
My Best Friend

Story Openers

I knew I was lost when . . .
The happiest I have ever been . . .
Nobody saw him do it, but . . .
My child is special because . . .
The trouble started when . . .
I was afraid to admit that . . .
Someone who changed my life was . . .
When the doorbell rang . . .
I promised to keep the secret, but . . .
The day my car broke down . . .
I am not afraid of . . .
The best party I remember was . . .
One place I never want to visit again is . . .
The strangest thing that ever happened to me was . . .
Help! He can't swim . . .
If I were filthy rich, I'd . . .
The letter never came from . . .
One thing that really bores me is . . .
I don't like . . .